NATI[...] GEO[...]

When Spring Comes

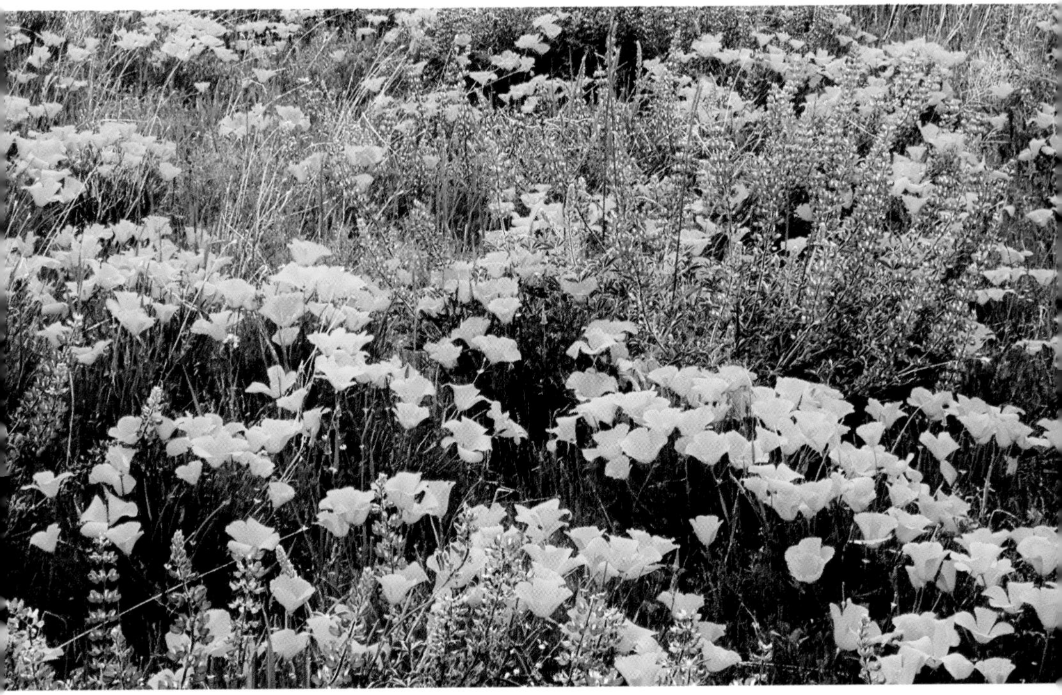

Solomon Gordon

When **spring** comes, snow melts.

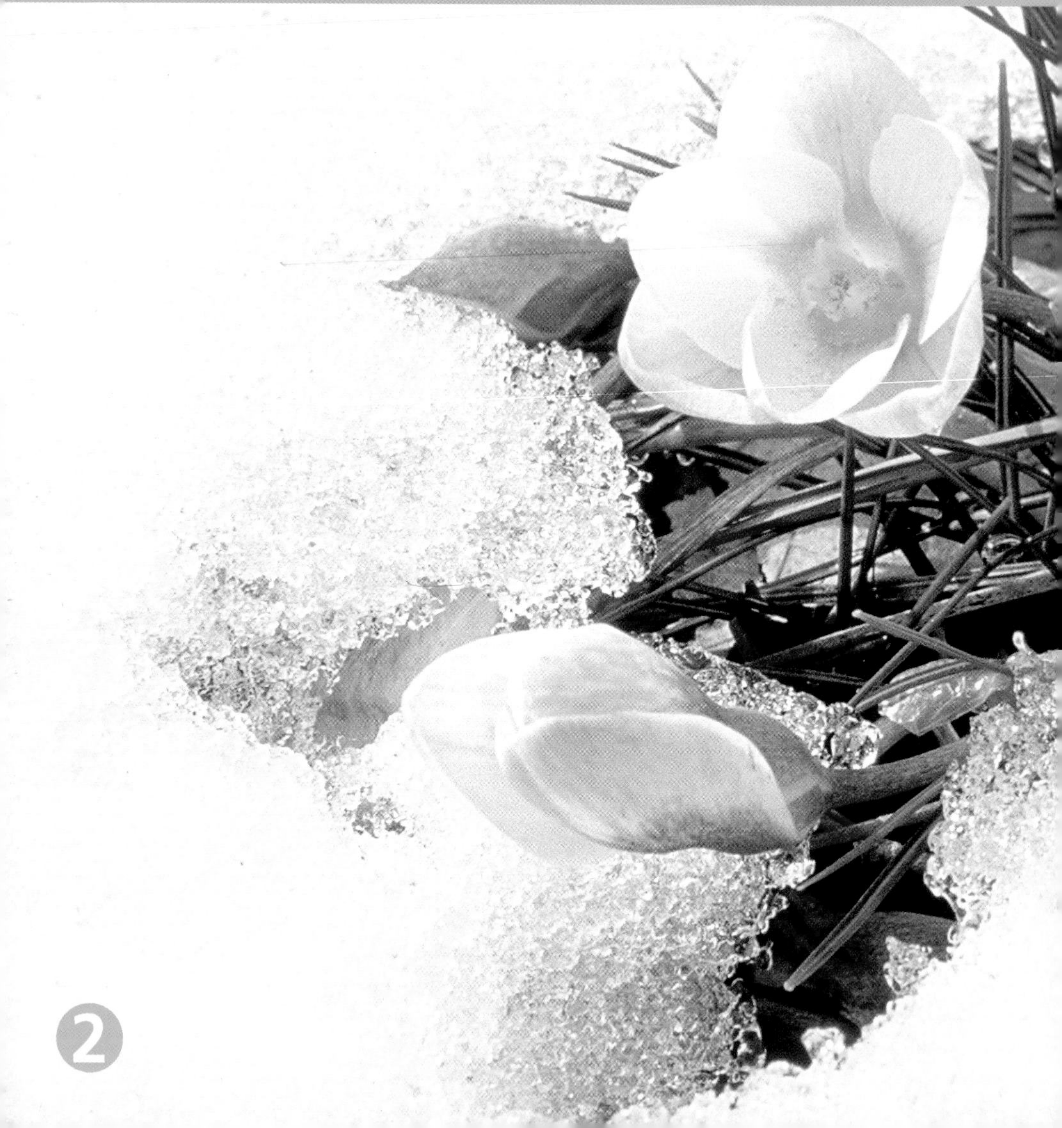

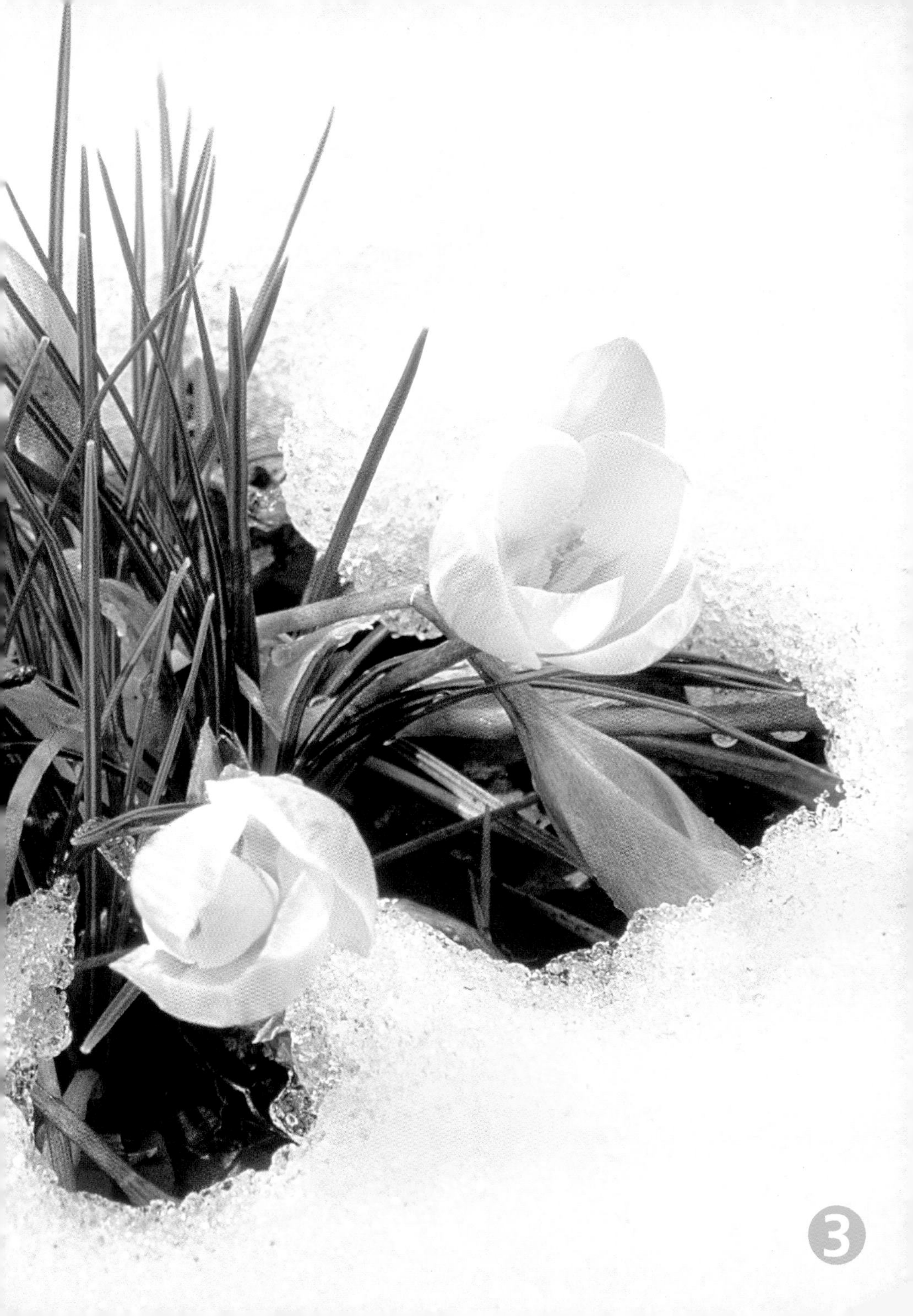

When **spring** comes, flowers bloom.

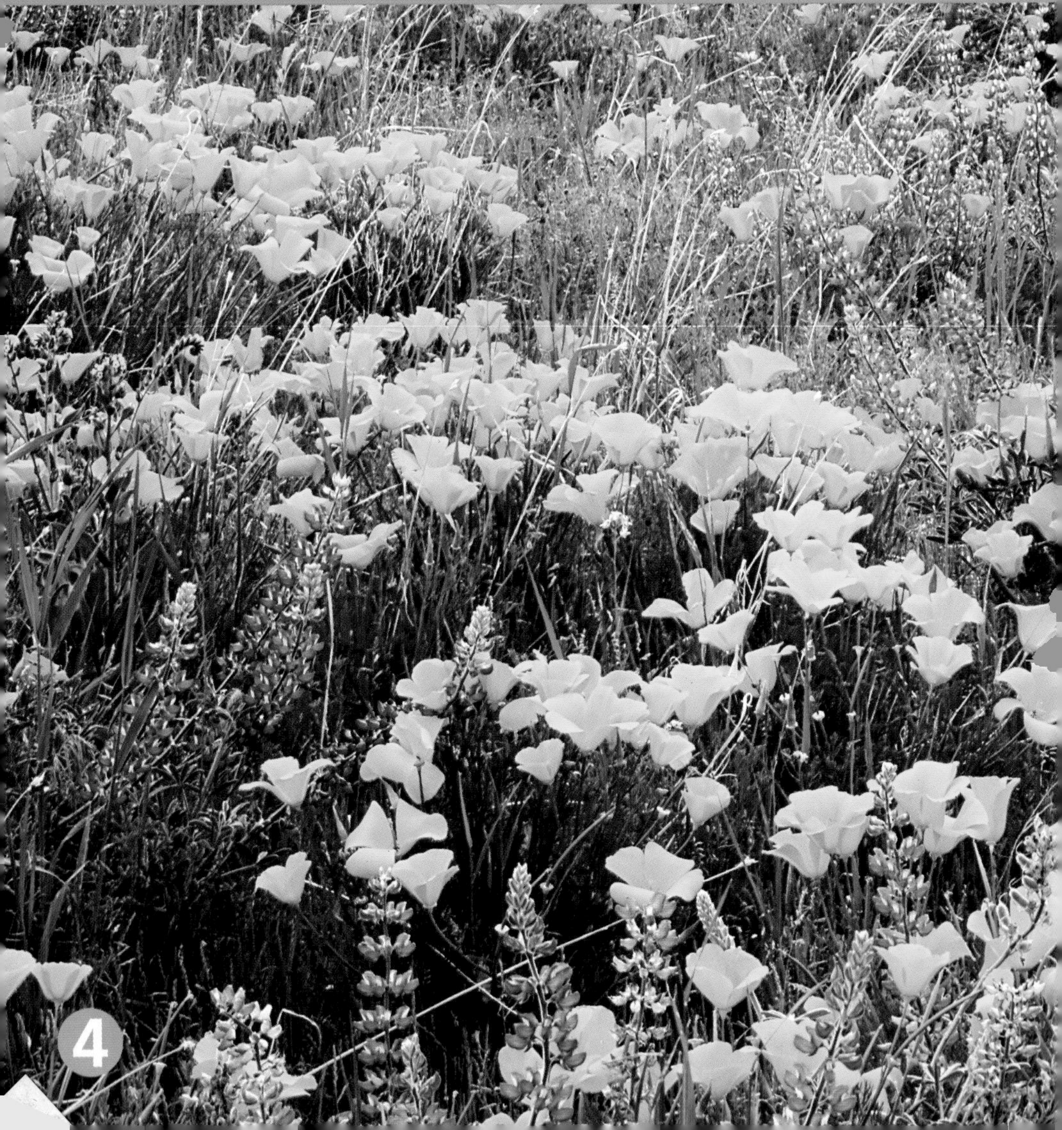

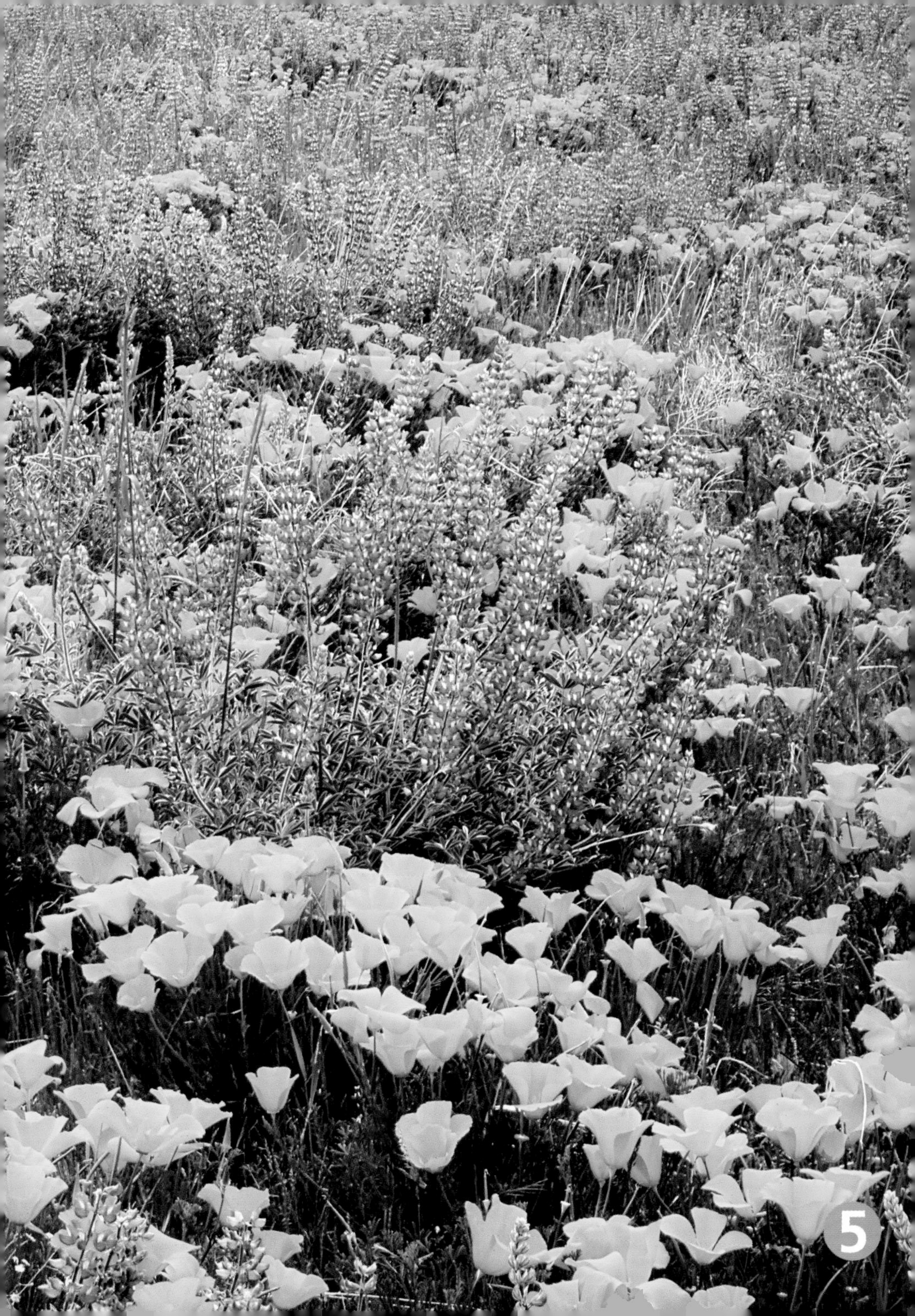

When **spring** comes, some animals wake up.

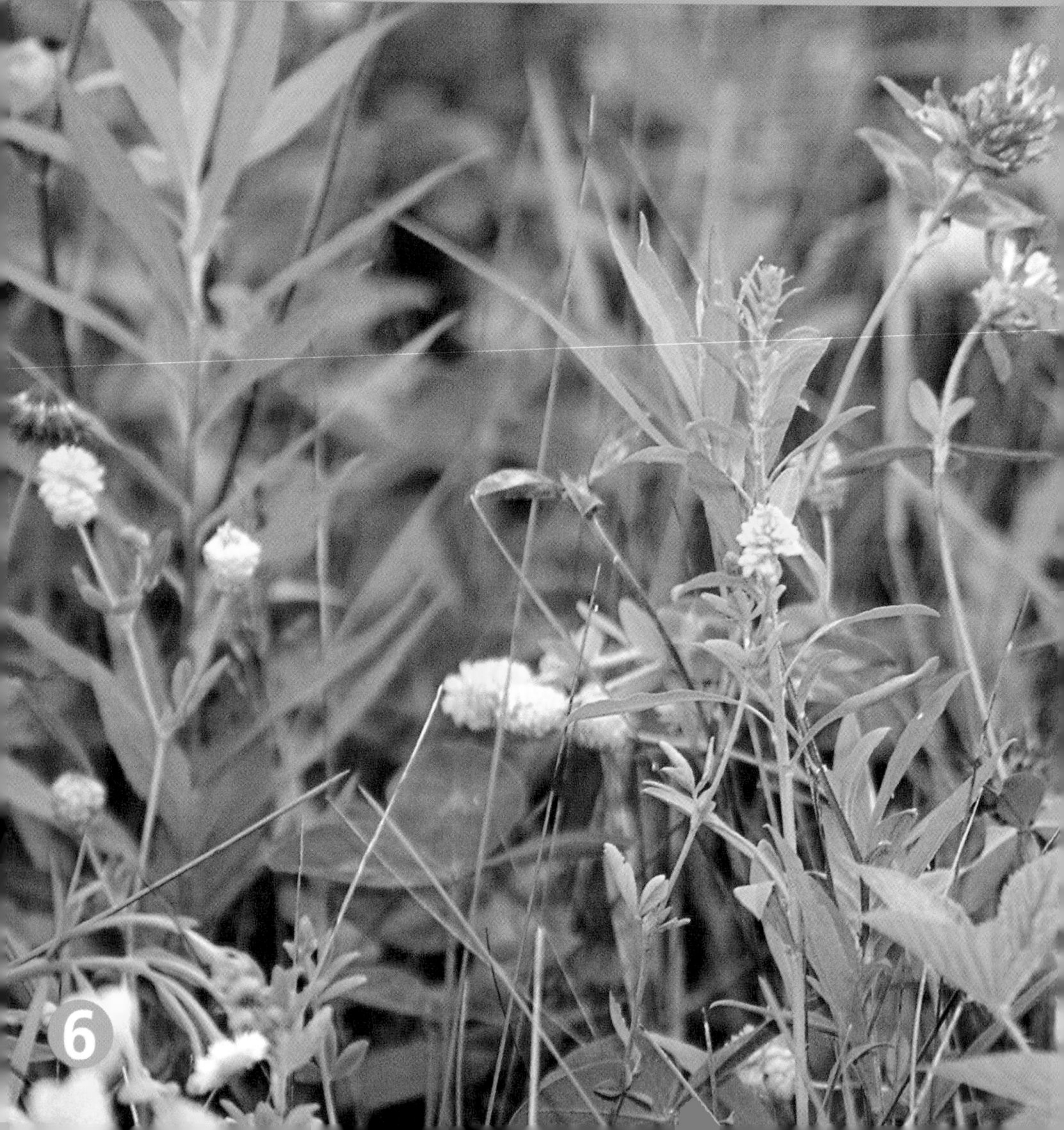

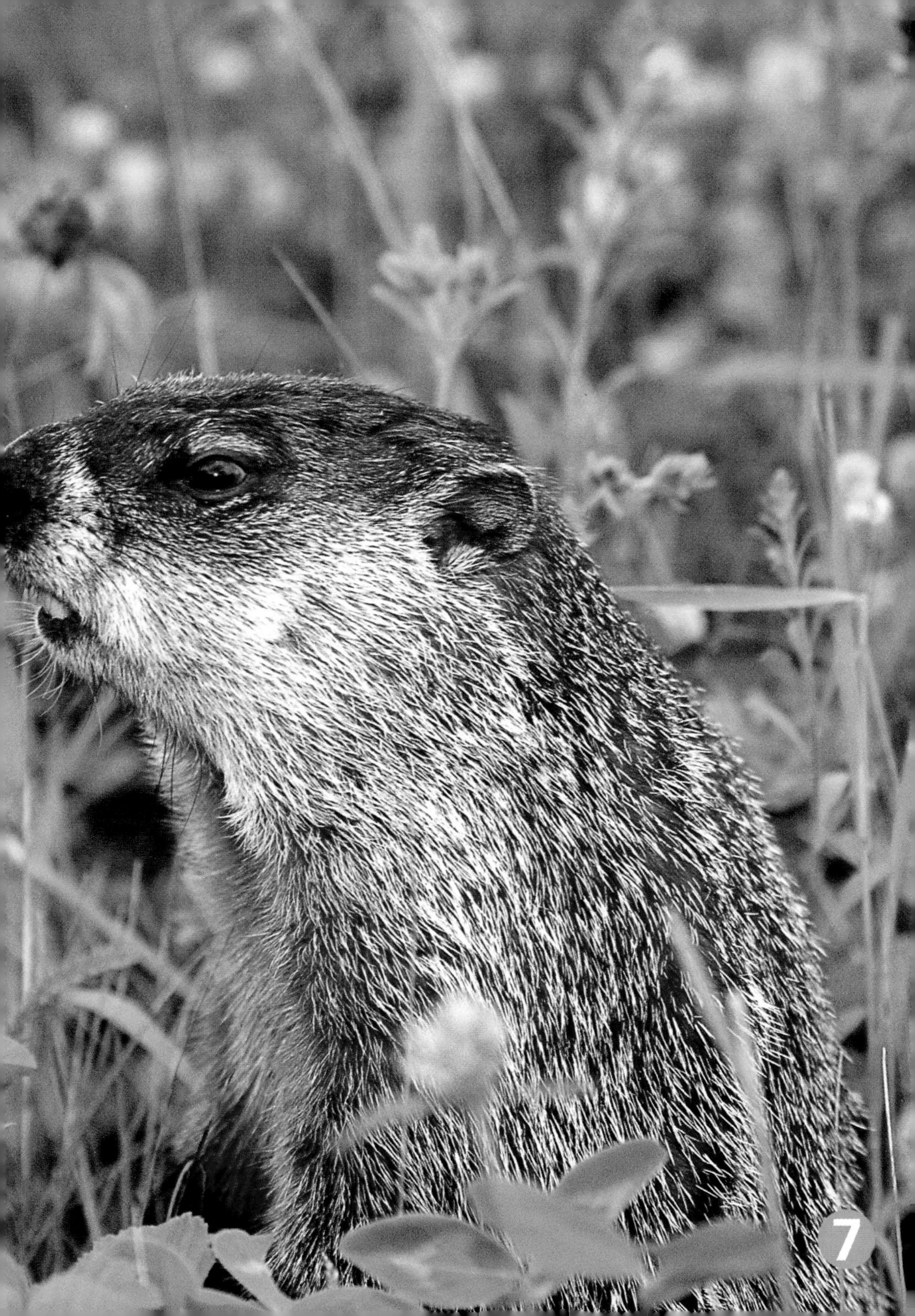

When **spring** comes,
I play outside.

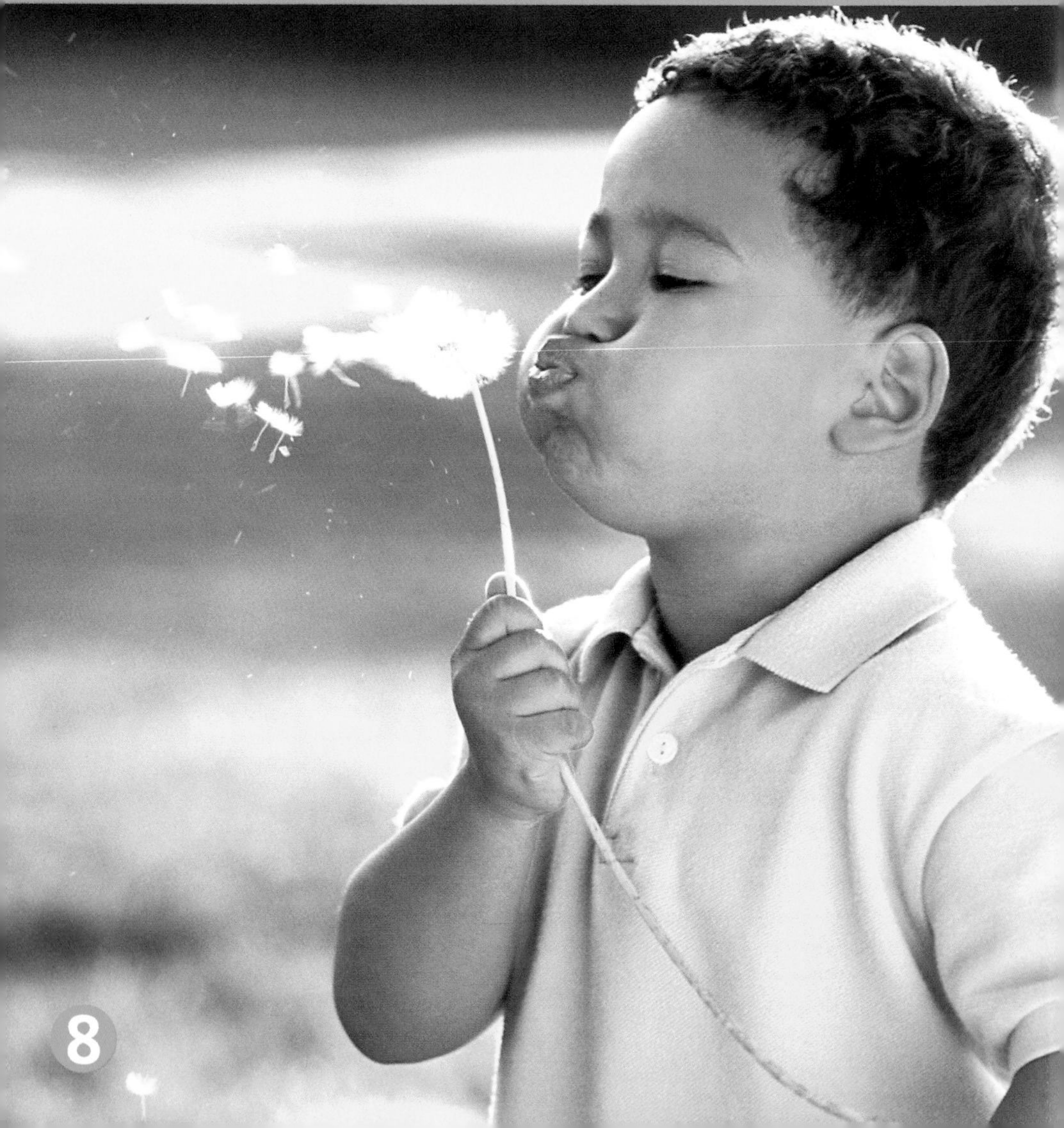